... for here there is no pla
change your life.
— Rainer Maria Rilkie, "Archaic Torso of Apollo"

Man is nothing else but what he makes of himself.
— Jean-Paul Sartre

Assume a virtue, if you have it not.
Refrain tonight,
And that shall lend a kind of easiness
To the next abstinence; the next more easy;
For use almost can change the stamp of nature.
— Shakespeare, *Hamlet*, Act 3. scene 4.

Tired of Yourself?

A Guide to Meaningful Change

Max Malikow

Tired of Yourself?

To Dean Olin: Whose change is remarkable and continuing.

To Charles Lunderman: Who trusted himself, went his own way, and is making a better life.

To Tracy Brown: Who I hope never changes.

Acknowledgments

Every book emerges from something. Concerning this one, 34 years of practicing psychotherapy have engaged me in intimate conversations with hundreds of individuals seeking to change in one way or another. It has been my privilege to have been part of these conversations. Not all of these people accomplished the change they desired, but nearly all of them made an effort and thereby contributed to my continuing education. This book would not have been possible without having encountered these patients and clients.

Lest I appear above the fray, I confess that my long-running curiosity about change has been sustained by my own numerous failures and sporadic successes at self-improvement. I am mindful of an adage popular among the clergy: "When you point a finger at your congregation, there are three more pointing back at you."

Preface

We are all much less than we can be.

- Leonard Buscaglia

With few exceptions, people who find their way to a psychotherapist's office want to investigate the possibility of change. And what is psychotherapy? It is engagement with a mental health professional to examine, understand, and possibly change thoughts, feelings, and/or behaviors. The following pages address change by responding to five questions:

1. What does it mean to change?

2. Why is change difficult?

3. How is change accomplished?

4. What is changeable and what isn't?

5. Why did an eminent psychiatrist not change?

E. Fuller Torrey maintains asking if psychotherapy works is like asking if prostitution works. He argues since both professions have a long history of providing service for a fee the proper question is not *if* they work but *how* they work.

While this is a clever way to approach the question of psychotherapy's effectiveness, longevity does not authenticate efficacy. Seances also have a long history but this does not validate them as a reliable means for communing with the dead. Prostitution offers an erotic experience, albeit without intimacy, and a seance provides the illusion of necromancy. The question concerning psychotherapy is whether it delivers on its promise of self-examination culminating in the possibility of change. The renowned (some would say notorious) psychiatrist Thomas Szasz takes up this question and writes:

> People seeking help from psychotherapists can be divided into two groups: those who wish to confront their difficulties and shortcomings and change their lives by changing themselves; and those who wish to avoid the inevitable consequences of their life strategies through the magical or tactical intervention of therapists in their lives. Those in the former group may derive great benefit from therapy in a few weeks or months; those in the latter may stand still, or sink even deeper into their self-created life morass, after meeting with psychotherapists for years, and even decades (1973, p. 109).

An Italian proverb, "Quando una persona fu nato rotundo, non puoi morire quadrata" translates to English as, "When a person is born round, he doesn't die square." If this is true then anyone attempting to change is on a fool's errand. Although I enjoy the linguistics of this adage I do not agree with its declaration. I believe people can change. However, change does not come easily. It requires realism, desire, motivation, commitment, planning, resilience, and, often, courage.

This is a book about change.

Max Malikow
Syracuse, NY
April 6, 2019

Table of Contents

Chapter I. What Does It Mean to Change?

Dear God I ain't what I wanna be.
And I ain't what I'm gonna be.
And I sure ain't what I oughta be.
But thank God I ain't what I used to be!

- Gert Behanna

Question: How many psychiatrists does it take to change a lightbulb? Answer: Only one, but the lightbulb really has to want to change.

Unlike lightbulbs, people often have the desire to change something about themselves. Moreover, among living things, human beings have the unique capacity to accomplish self-change. The possibility of physical change is not the subject of this book. That people can change their bodies through diet and exercise, as well as cosmetic surgery is indisputable. The American Society of Plastic Surgeons reports approximately 18 million cosmetic surgical and minimally invasive procedures performed in 2018 (Townley, 2019). The interest of this book is nonphysical changes in thinking, feeling, and behaving.

Synonyms for change include *alter, vary, modify, transform,* and *convert. Rehabilitate* is not usually synonymous with *change*, but the two words are equivalent in the context of a scene from the movie, "The Shawshank Redemption," based on the Stephen King novella, *Rita Hayworth and Shawshank Redemption*. In one scene a convict named Ellis Boyd Redding is interviewed by the parole board for consideration for release from prison. The interview begins with him being asked if he has been rehabilitated. Redding, who has served 40 years of a life sentence, responds, "Rehabilitated? Well now, let me see. You know, come to think of it, I have no idea what that means" (1994). When one of the board members begins to offer a definition Redding interrupts and continues:

> I know what you think it means, Sonny. Me? I think it's a made-up word, a politician's word, so young fellas like you can wear a suit and tie and have a job. What do you really want to know? Am I sorry for what I did? ... Not a day goes by I don't feel regret; not because I'm in here or because you think I should. I look back on the way I was then...that young, stupid kid who committed that terrible crime. ...I want to try to talk some sense to him, tell him how things are. But I can't. That kid's long gone, this old man is all that's left. I have to live with that. Rehabilitated? That's just a bullshit word. So you just go on ahead and stamp your form there, Sonny, and stop wasting my time. To tell you the truth, I don't give a shit (1994).

Oscar Wilde, writes, "With age comes wisdom but sometimes age comes alone" (2019). In Ellis Boyd Redding's case old age did not arrive unaccompanied. It was 40 years of reflection, not 40 years of incarceration, that changed his worldview. For those who are reflective, wisdom can be the consolation prize of aging.

In another movie, this one quite forgettable, martial artist Steven Seagal administers a dreadful beating to a bully. At the end of the beating Seagal asks the bad guy, "What does it take to change the essence of a man?" Battered and bleeding, the bully responds, "Time, it takes time to change" (1994). Even given time, the essence of a person rarely changes? A person's essence or inherent nature is that individual's personality – the pattern of thinking, feeling, behaving, and relating that characterizes that person. Personality is the product of genetics and experiences ("nature and nurture") and crystallized well before adolescence. With the exception of a profound life experience a personality does not change. (These rare exceptions are addressed in chapter III.) Psychologist Robert Wright writes of the persistence of personality in his bestseller *Why Buddhism Is True*:

> When I think of myself, I think of something that *persists through time*. I've changed a lot since I was ten years old, but hasn't some inner essence – my identity, my self - in some sense endured? Isn't that the one constant amid the flux? (2017, p. 63).

In contrast to personality, specific thoughts, feelings, and behaviors can be targeted for change. These changes are deliberate rather than serendipitous. A phrase associated with alcohol addiction and recovery is the "dry drunk," referring to the alcoholic who stops drinking but retains the personality that preceded the alcoholism and, likely, contributed to it. The title of this book asks, "Tired of yourself?" People become tired of themselves because of unwanted thoughts, feelings, and/or behaviors rather than personality. Essayist Meghan Daum's observation succinctly expresses this reality: "Life is mostly an exercise in being something other than we used to be while remaining fundamentally – and sometimes maddenmaddeningly ¬ who we are" (Popova, 2014, p.9). The following pages are concerned with intentional changes in thinking, feeling, and behaving, not personality transformation.

Chapter II. Why Is Change Difficult?

We have met the enemy and he is us.

- Walt Kelly

The frontal cortex is the part of the brain that enables us to do the harder thing.

- Robert Sapolsky

In a comedy skit Bob Newhart portrays a caricature of a psychologist whose therapy sessions last no longer than five minutes because all he does is berate his patients and tell them to, "Stop it!" People do not change because someone has scornfully admonished them. Neither does change occur because of information, regardless of its trustworthiness. A *Time Magazine* cover story ("Ten Foods that Pack a Wallop") features ten foods a consensus of experts on nutrition agree should be a part of everyone's diet (Horowitz, 2002, pp. 76-81):

broccoli
blueberries
garlic
green tea
nuts
oats
red wine
salmon

spinach

tomatoes

After presenting this information to my students I ask them if they agree with the experts. Invariably they have trusted the information but when asked if it will have any influence on their diet they say it will not. Similarly, the warning given on a pack of cigarettes ("Caution: Cigarette Smoking May Be Hazardous to Your Health") is trustworthy information that is largely disregarded. While information can be useful it is often insufficient to effect change.

Another "change" exercise for my students is an assignment in which they are given 15 weeks to change a behavior of their choice. (Fifteen weeks is the length of a semester and they choose the behavior in the first week.) The behavior can be something they want to stop or something they want to start. Over the years I have tracked their success rate and it is approximately ten percent. What accounts for their 90 percent rate of failure? The answer lies in their motivation for change. The initiative for the change was an academic assignment (an extrinsic motivator) rather than a self-determined need to change (an intrinsic motivator). Also, their grade was not determined by success in making the change but from two writing assignments. Hence, there were no "real-life" consequences for failure. There is no sense of urgency associated with this assignment. As T.S. Eliot observed, "One starts an action simply because one must do something" (1959, p. 38).

Moreover, even the simplest of changes can cause discomfort. Try folding your arms the opposite way or brushing your teeth with your left hand if you're right-handed. More challenging is cursively writing your signature ten times with the opposite hand. Likely the signature will improve until fatigue sets in causing it to deteriorate. (The fatigue results from concentrating on a task previously performed without thinking.)

Albert Ellis, one of the twentieth century's most influential psychologists, offers an analysis of why people fail at change:

> The main reason people stay in jobs they hate, relationships that are abusive, friendships that are critical, and continue to smoke and drink addictively is low frustration tolerance - things must be easy. They say to themselves, "Even though it's desirable for me to change in the long run, it's going to be very hard in the short run and therefore I'll do it tomorrow, I'll do it tomorrow, I'll do it tomorrow."
>
> The other reason for procrastinating about change is fear of failure. "If I change I must have a guarantee that it will work out, everything will be fine, I will succeed, and people will love me. Since I don't have that guarantee, particularly in a new situation, I'll do it tomorrow or I won't do it at all."
>
> A subheading under fear of failure is fear of disapproval.

Now, it is human to stick with what is known. You choose to drive a car with or without a stick shift. You know it, it's easy. You're habituated to it. You're successful. Most of the things you do you know how to handle. People do what's easy and what's guaranteed rather than what's hard even though it would give them greater pleasure and greater success down the road. Most people are short-range hedonists. They go for the pleasure of the moment rather than look into the future (Wholey, 1997, p. 45).

Thomas Szasz writes of learning in a way that often applies to changing. (Substitute "change" for "learn" in the following quotation to appreciate this similarity.)

Every act of conscious learning requires the willingness to suffer an injury to one's self-esteem. This is why young children, before they are aware of their own self-importance, learn so easily; and why older persons, especially if vain or important, cannot learn at all (1973, p. 18).

Often a desire to change is simultaneously an acknowledgment of error. To admit to being wrong, especially to admit to having been wrong for a long time, requires a willingness to suffer an injury to one's ego. This requires courage, which Szasz believes is a prerequisite for change: "Success in psychotherapy - that is, the ability to change oneself in a direction in which one wants to change - requires courage rather than insight" (p. 109).

This chapter describes why change is difficult. Thus far, the difficulty has been explained in terms of tactics that do not work (admonishment, information, and extrinsic motivation) and inhibitors (discomfort, low frustration tolerance, fear of failure, fear of disapproval, pride, and lack of courage). The length of this list notwithstanding, an analysis of the difficulty of change would be incomplete if it did not include the capacity to make peace with failure. The 90 percent of students in the behavioral change assignment who did not succeed explained their failure in one of three ways, each beginning with the letter "R." Some students *reevaluated* their chosen behavior and, like a professional football referee, reported, "Upon further review the original call has been overturned." After reconsidering their choice they decided they didn't want to change their selected behavior. Other students *resigned* themselves to a lifetime with an unwanted behavior. They admitted to their inability to change and, like the comedian Steve Allen, conceded, "I am loyal to a fault; I have many faults and I am loyal to all of them" (Malikow, 2014, p. 28). Still other students *rationalized* their failure as a favorable outcome. They argued the behavior they thought they wanted to change was actually something they wanted to continue because they came to see it as an asset rather than a liability. (Note: *Rationalizing* is irrational excuse-making, often defending something bad through flawed reasoning. One of Freud's ten defense mechanisms, it operates unconsciously to reduce anxiety.)

Chapter III. How Is Change Accomplished?

I went to a bookstore and asked the saleswoman, "Where's the self-help section?" She said if she told me, it would defeat the purpose.

- Steve Wright

Gene Kranz was the NASA Flight Director for the 1970 Apollo-13 manned spaceflight. The mission was to land on the moon. When an oxygen tank exploded in the service module the mission was aborted and replaced by the task of getting the three man crew back to earth. This required exceptional ingenuity on the part of the engineers on the ground under Kranz's supervision. His memoir of the successful second mission is titled *Failure Is Not an Option* (2009). Rarely do life and death depend on change, but when they do "failure is not an option." Recall T.S. Eliot's observation, "One starts an action simply because one must do something" (1959, p. 38). Former professional golfer Laura Baugh began her sobriety simply because she had to do something or die:

> Only when blood seeped from her eyes, nose, and fingernails did Laura Baugh realize she might die.
> It was only when the platelets in her blood ceased clotting and she bled uncontrollably, internally and

externally, that Baugh was ready to admit she was an alcoholic. ... To drink again was to die (Becker, 1997).

Baugh, a mother of six at the time her recovery began, has been "clean and sober" for over 20 years. Concerning her sobriety she believes, "Nobody made me drink, and nobody can make you get sober. You have to want to do it yourself. You can want to get sober for your children, but you have to want to get sober for yourself" (1997). When she thinks about drinking she reminds herself of how close she came to dying: "I think about alcohol at the darnedest times. What I do then is follow that last drink through and remember the platelets and the bleeding. That's why I'm lucky to have that memory. It keeps me sober" (1997).

Laura Baugh's confrontation with death was a "rock bottom" experience. Addicts arrive at "rock bottom" in different ways. Abraham Twerski, a psychiatrist, rabbi, and expert on substance abuse treatment, elaborates on "rock bottom" in recovery:

> The term "rock bottom" has been traditionally used and is still widely used in the addiction field, so it is just as well to preserve it. However, it should be clarified. "Rock bottom" does not necessarily mean total desocialization, loss of family, or loss of employment; it does not mean utter disaster. All it means is something has occurred in the life of the addict that has

sufficient impact to make the addict wish to change at least part of his or her lifestyle (1997, p. 101).

Psychologist Howard Gardner agrees,

> What happens when we change our minds? And exactly what does it take for a person to change her mind and begin to act on the basis of this shift? Our minds are changed either because we ourselves want to change them or because something happens in our mental life that warrants a change (2004, p. 1).

Ed Rosenbaum changed his mind because of an experience and acted differently because of it. A physician, he became a patient when diagnosed with laryngeal cancer at age 70. Depending on doctors, being misdiagnosed, and undergoing treatment with an uncertain outcome made for a life-changing experience. Prior to his illness he believed in maintaining the professional distance from his patients accordant with his training. Rosenbaum was so proficient at this that he seemed indifferent to them. His experience with cancer not only changed him, it moved him to write a memoir, *A Taste of My Own Medicine: When the Doctor Is the Patient* (1988). The success of his book and the movie derived from it led him to pursue a second career as an advocate for more humane practices in medicine. Upon his death in 2009 his son Jim, also a physician, said, "He left a legacy and changed the way physicians practice" (Beaven, 2009).

The experience of a single encounter also can ignite change. Granted, Victor Hugo's *Les Miserables* is a novel, but there is a reason for its universal appeal for over 150 years. (It also has been produced as a movie three times and its musical version is the second longest running musical in theatrical history.) The explanation for its ubiquitous acclaim is the odyssey of its protagonist, Jean Valjean. A hardened ex-convict concerned only with survival, his encounter with a priest who extends kindness redirects Valjean's life. Like Valjean, everyone is in some way indebted to others. Albert Einstein believed this and wrote:

> From the standpoint of daily life ... there is one thing we do know: that man is here for the sake of other men - above all for those upon whose smile and well-being our own happiness depends, and also for the countless unknown souls with whose fate we are connected by a bond of sympathy. Many times a day I realize how much of my own outer and inner life is built upon the labors of my fellow men, both living and dead, and how earnestly I must exert myself in order to give in return as much as I have received (1990, p. 202).

Change sometimes results from serendipitous insight. This happened to the writer Augusten Burroughs as he was preparing to commit suicide:

> I realized suicide was the last thing I wanted to do.

It was actually the opposite of what I desired. Suicide would not accomplish any of my goals. ...

When I saw it this way I realized something. It wasn't that I wanted to kill myself.

What I really wanted was to end my life.

I hadn't been able to make the distinction before really thinking it through. Ending my life didn't mean I had to die.

It meant I could change my name from *Chris* to something more alphabet-dominant and with numerous syllables, not just the measly one. Something with the subtle sheen of celebrity to it. *Augusten.* ...

Oh yes, I could. If I ended my life, I could start another one. Where things did not happen to me, but I made them happen.

Just because most people never even think to step outside their life didn't mean I couldn't do exactly that.

This little speck of western Massachusetts was the only place I had ever known. But it was not the only place.

What did I really and truly need in order to be reborn?

Maybe just two things. A door. And then a highway. ...

When your life reaches the state of emergency and the only thing you can think to do is end it, maybe the thing to do is break it.

Walk out the door.

So I did (2012, pp. 99-100).

Unanticipated insight also came to the renowned attorney Gerry Spence. After agonizing over whether to divorce in order to marry another woman, he decided he would. That decision made, he realized another change would be necessary. He and his new wife, Imaging, would have to stop drinking:

> That was 1969, and within days after my divorce, Imaging and I had run off to Tahoe to get married. I used to laugh about it - just as well - that I've been unmarried only nine days in my entire adult life. The Sunday morning shrinks would have said I escaped one trap only to fall into another. But a trap of love is not a trap. It's heaven with a fence around it. Imaging changed my life. ...
>
> "We gotta make this work, Imaging," I said. "If we don't, we've screwed ourselves good."
>
> "And everybody else," she said. If love meant anything it had to be responsible - we said things like that. I knew the booze was in the way. She knew it, too. The booze was dangerous, it had to go. ...
>
> "Strange life without the booze, like losing an old friend," I said.
>
> "We have to find new friends. If you aren't drunk with your old friends you can't stand'em anymore, " Imaging said (Spence, 1996, pp. 419-420).

Not drinking required yet another change - new friends. Hence, one change (divorce) led to two others.

"Another Woman" is not the kind of movie usually associated with Woody Allen, its writer and director. Serious and probing, it's the story of a middle-aged philosophy professor, Marion Post, who is confronted with unflattering observations about her made by several people who know her well. Surprised to learn these people experience her as aloof and self-serving, she is driven to conclude she is not the person she has long believed herself to be. Near the movie's end, when reading a Rainer Maria Rilke poem, "Archaic Torso of Apollo," she is moved to tears as she reads: "... for here there is no place that does not see you. You must change your life" (1918). She resolves to change and takes it upon herself to become a more benevolent person.

Marion was awakened and shocked by the *convergent data* that confronted her. Convergent data is information derived from independent sources. It can be favorable or unfavorable information. In Marion's case, it was the latter. Convergent data accounts for why "interventions" can be successful in convincing addicts they need to change. In an intervention an addict is confronted with the effect the addictive behavior has on significant people in the addict's life. When successful, an awakening occurs and a commitment to change follows.

As given in the preface, the definition of psychotherapy is engagement with a mental health professional to examine, understand, and possibly change thoughts, feelings, and/or behaviors. There are many "schools" or "theories" of psychotherapy and while many are related, many are independent of all the others. One of the newer approaches built upon earlier, more established theories is *cognitive behavioral therapy* (CBT). Developed by psychiatrist Aaron T. Beck, it is derived from *behavioral theory*, originated by Ivan Pavlov, and *rational emotive behavioral therapy*, developed by Albert Ellis. CBT is based on the assumption that some mental health problems derive from negative thoughts that are illogical and unsupportable. Beck coined the term "cognitive triad" for the unwarranted beliefs many troubled people have concerning themselves, the world, and the future. Drawing illogical conclusions and believing things that cannot stand up to scrutiny make life excessively arduous and exhausting. Beck does not posit all negative thoughts are groundless; only those that are baseless are challenged in CBT. Like Socrates, Beck believes an examined life is the best possible life. While CBT is not suitable for addressing all of life's issues it can be an effective approach for some clients.

Also stated in the preface is the belief that people can change. (The subtitle of this book is *A Guide to Meaningful Change*.) Still, change does not come easily. It typically requires commitment to a well-considered strategy as well as the courage to accept some unpleasant realities and forsake some long-held beliefs.

There is nothing positive about guilt if it results only in self-flagellation. But when deep regret for a misdeed propels self-improvement then guilt is redemptive. Psychiatrist and Holocaust survivor Viktor Frankl writes optimistically about guilt in *Man's Search for Meaning*, characterizing it as an "opportunity to change one's self for the better" (1984, p. 162). When speaking to inmates at San Quentin he told them,

> You are human beings, like me, and as such you were free to commit a crime, to become guilty. Now, however, you are responsible for overcoming guilt by rising above it, by growing beyond yourselves, by changing for the better (2004, p. 149).

Freud also believed in the redemptive possibility of guilt. He posited the development of a conscience (the superego) makes possible the experience of guilt which, in turn, can lead to moral self-improvement:

> A great change takes place ... through the establishment of a superego ... it is not until now that we should speak of conscience or sense of guilt. At this point the fear of being found out comes to an end; the distinction moreover, between doing something bad and wishing to do it disappears entirely, since nothing can be hidden from the superego, not even thoughts (1961, p. 86).

A religious experience is yet another impetus for change. In the New Testament gospels Jesus is engaged in a conversation with Nicodemus, a Jewish religious scholar. Their dialogue features the well-known term "born again:"

Now there was a man of the Pharisees named Nicodemus, a member of the Jewish ruling council. He came to Jesus at night and said, "Rabbi, we know you are a teacher who has come from God. For no one could perform the miraculous signs you are doing if God were not with him.

In reply Jesus declared, "I tell you the truth, no one can see the kingdom of God unless he is born again."

"How can a man be born when he is old?" Nicodemus asked. "Surely he cannot enter a second time into his mother's womb to be born!"

Jesus answered, "I tell you the truth, no one can enter the kingdom of God unless he is born of water and the Spirit. Flesh gives birth to flesh, but the Spirit gives birth to spirit. You should not be surprised at my saying, 'You must be born again.' The wind blows wherever it pleases. You can hear its sound, but you cannot tell where it comes from or where it is going. So it is with everyone born of the Spirit (John 3: 1-8, NIV).

This is a conversation between two rabbis. Nicodemus is a member of the Jewish ruling council (the Sanhedrin) and Jesus an itinerating teacher. Typical of such conversations, it takes the form of "question-and-answer." Jesus states entrance into the kingdom of God requires a "born again" experience. Nicodemus responds with the impossibility of a man reentering into his mother's womb in order to have a second birth. In turn, Jesus responds that the second birth is not physical, but spiritual, and it is the spiritual birth that makes a person sensitive to the voice and will of God. In the New Testament's original language, Greek, *gennao anothen* is translated "born again." But *gennao anothen* also could be translated "born from above." Given Jesus' intention, either translation is acceptable.

According to Christian theology, being made alive to God results in a radically altered worldview and reordered life. This is what the Apostle Paul had in mind when he wrote, "Therefore, if anyone is in Christ, he is a new creation; the old has gone, the new has come" (2 Corinthians 5:17, NIV). This idea is reinforced by considering the Greek behind the word "new." There are two Greek words for "new," *neos* and *kainos*. The former means "recent; another of the same kind." The latter, which is the word found in 2 Corinthians 5:17, means "new in quality; new and different; implying a superior innovation or advance" (Hill, 1987, p. 541). Some, but certainly not all, "born again" experiences result in a changed personality. Chapter I ("What does it mean to change?") includes the assertion that an individual's personality does not change, except in rare instances. The balance of this chapter addresses the rare instance of a changed personality. (Recall from chapter I that personality is an individual's characteristic pattern of thinking, feeling, acting, and relating to others.)

William James, renowned as a psychologist and philosopher, defined religion as, "the belief that there is an unseen order, and that our supreme good lies in harmoniously adjusting ourselves thereto" (1902, p. 53). In his celebrated collection of lectures analyzing religious experiences he devoted one lecture to religious conversion in which he said, "To say that a man is 'converted' means ... that religious ideas, previously peripheral in his consciousness, now take a central place, and that religious aims form the habitual centre of his energy" (James, 1902, p.193). An excellent illustration of *kainos* and James' understanding of conversion is found in Charles Dickens' *A Christmas Carol*. Ebenezer Scrooge, upon seeing his name etched on a gravestone, is overwhelmed by the realization that he is going to die unacknowledged at the end of his insignificant life. He learns this from the last of the visiting spirits, the Ghost of Christmas Yet to Come:

"Spirit!" he cried, tight clutching at its robe, "hear me! I am not the man I was. I will not be the man I must have been but for this intercourse. Why show me this, if I am past all hope?"

For the first time the hand appeared to shake.

"Good Spirit," he pursued as he fell before it: "Your nature intercedes for me, and pities me. Assure me that I yet may change these shadows you have shown me, by an altered life!" The kind hand trembled.

"I will honor Christmas in my heart, and try to keep it all the year. I will live in the Past, the Present, and the Future. The Spirits of all Three shall strive within me. I will not shut out the lessons that they teach. Oh, tell me I may sponge away the writing on this stone!" (Dickens, 2013, p. 102).

The story ends with a description of Scrooge as the epitome of *kainos*:

> Scrooge was better than his word. He did it all, and infinitely more ...He lived upon the Total Abstinence Principle, ever afterwards; and it was always said of him, that he knew how to keep Christmas well, if any man alive possessed the knowledge (p. 111).

William James may have had Ebenezer Scrooge in mind when he wrote, "Psychology and religion ... both admit that there are forces seemingly outside of the conscious individual that bring redemption to his life" (1902, p. 207). If not Scrooge, James had several real-life individuals in mind and offered them as examples of a radically reordered life. One of them, Alphonse Rattisbonne, provided a description of his conversion: "I did not know if I was Alphonse or another. I only felt myself changed and believed myself another me; I looked for myself in myself and did not find myself" (p. 221).

A contemporary example of a changed personality is Chuck Colson. Once known as President Nixon's "hatchet man" and an "evil genius," Colson was involved in the infamous Watergate break-in and served seven months in a federal prison for obstruction of justice. The year before his incarceration he embraced Christianity and radically reordered his life. Thirty years later *Time* magazine recognized him as one of the 25 most influential evangelical Christians in America (2005). He founded several non-profit Christian ministries, including the Prison Fellowship and the Prison Fellowship International. Before his death in 2012 he had received 15 honorary doctorates, a Templeton Prize for Progress in Religion (awarded for an exceptional contribution to affirming a spiritual worldview), and a Presidential Citizens Medal. He donated the one million dollar Templeton Prize, royalties from his 30 books, and all his speaker's fees to the Prison Fellowship ministry.

Chapter IV. What Is Changeable and What Isn't

A man's got to know his limitations.
> - Harry Callahan (Clint Eastwood)

In *What You Can Change and What You Can't: The Complete Guide to Successful Self-Improvement* the eminent psychologist Martin Seligman writes:

> Millions are struggling to change: We diet, we jog, we meditate. We adopt new modes of thought to counteract our depressions. We practice relaxation to curb our distress. Sometimes it works. But distressingly often, self-improvement and psycho-therapy fail. The cost is enormous. We think we are worthless. We feel guilty and ashamed. We believe we have no willpower and that we are failures. We give up trying to change (1993, p. 3).

Seligman believes many failures at self-improvement result from misguided attempts to change the unchangeable. True to the title of his book, he classifies attempts to change into two categories: the possible (what you can change) and the impossible (what you can't). His suggestion corresponds to a teaching of *stoicism*, a philosophy which instructs asking, in every circumstance, "Can I control or, at least, influence this situation?" Epictetus, a second century stoic philosopher, taught, "There is only one way to happiness and that is to cease worrying about things which are beyond the power of our will" (2019).

Stoicism was put to the test by James Bond Stockdale, a prisoner of war in North Vietnam for seven and one-half years (four years in solitary confinement). After his release he was awarded the Congressional Medal of Honor, appointed President of the United States Naval War College, and served as President of The Citadel, the Military College of South Carolina. Stockdale credits his survival as a POW to Epictetus. After parachuting from his disabled Skyhawk fighter and "drifting along in a silence interrupted only by the whizz of bullets that luckily passed by me only to tear holes in the parachute canopy above me" Stockdale said to himself, "You are leaving the world of technology and entering the world of Epictetus" (Bennett, 1993, p. 517). Over the next nearly eight years these words of Epictetus sustained Stockdale: "There are things which are within your power, and there are things which are beyond your power. Concern yourself only with what is within your power" (p. 517).

During his captivity Stockdale kept *hope* separate from *expectation*. While he maintained hope that he would one day be liberated he did not expect it to happen soon or on any specific day:

> I never lost faith in the end of the story, I never doubted not only that I would get out, but also that I

would prevail in the end and turn the experience into the defining event of my life, which, in retrospect, I would not trade (Doherty, 2018 p. 1).

When asked why some did not survive the POW experience he said,

> Oh, that's easy, the optimists. Oh, they were the ones who said, 'We're going to be out by Christmas.' And Christmas would come, and Christmas would go. Then they'd say, 'We're going to be out by Easter.' And Easter would come, and Easter would go. And then Thanksgiving, and then it would be Christmas again. And they died of a broken heart (p.1).

This distinction between hope and expectation has been referred to as the "Stockdale Paradox," a phrase coined by Jim Collins, author of *Good to Great*, to describe one of the six characteristics of "good" businesses that become "great" (2001). Great businesses confront brutal facts without losing faith in eventual success. Collins acquired this concept from an interview with Stockdale who said,

> This is a very important lesson. You must never confuse faith that you will prevail in the end - which you can never afford to lose - with the discipline to confront the most brutal facts of your current reality, whatever they might be (2018, p.1).

Hope directs individuals to address the world as they would like it to be; expectation directs them to confront the world as it is, including its harsh realities. Everyone who buys a Mega Millions lottery ticket hopes to win but hardly anyone expects to. Seligman speaks similarly about realistic expectations when he offers five facts about what is changeable and five facts about what isn't. Concerning the former he believes:

1. Panic can be easily unlearned, but cannot be cured by medication.

2. The sexual dysfunctions¬frigidity, impotence, premature ejaculation–are easily unlearned.

3. Our moods, which can wreak havoc with our physical health, are readily controlled.

4. Depression can be cured by straightforward changes in conscious thinking and medication, but it cannot be cured by insight into childhood.

5. Optimism is a learned skill. Once learned, it increases achievement at work and improves physical health (1993, p. 5).

Concerning the latter he believes:

Tired of Yourself?

1. Dieting, in the long run, almost never works. Advice to the overweight: think fitness over fatness; pay attention to the makeup of your diet, and eat only when you're hungry.

2. Kids do not become *androgynous* (having the characteristics or nature of both male and female) easily.

3. No treatment is known to improve on the natural course of recovery from alcoholism.

Natural courses include a substitute dependency, painful medical consequences, a new source of hope (e.g. religious conversion), a new love relationship (that does not involve alcohol).

4. Homosexuality does not become heterosexuality.

5. Reliving childhood trauma does not undo adult personality problems (p. 5).

More often than not, change is not accomplished easily. Even the possible requires deliberation, determination, self-discipline, patience, planning, and self-knowledge:

1. Change begins with knowing and appreciating *why* the change is desirable. Determination comes from the conviction that the change will be life-enriching, if not life-saving. The

desire to change can arise as an impulse; sustaining that desire requires being fully convinced the prize is worth the effort.

2. Patience is the ability to endure under difficult circumstances - simply stated, it is the ability to wait. Self-discipline is the ability to control emotions and conduct. Patience and self-discipline are not synonymous, but they are interdependent. Shakespeare commends patience when he writes: "How poor are they that have not patience! What wound did ever heal but by degrees?"(*Othello*, Act 3, scene 2). Nearly always, change is a process. How poor are they who want to change but have not patience.

3. There is nothing magical about change. Shakespeare also writes: "Thou knowest we work by wit, and not by witchcraft, and wit depends on dilatory time." (*Othello*, Act 3, scene 2). This is an elegant expression of the idea that accomplishments result from plans, which take time to develop and execute. This same thought is expressed by an adage attributed to Benjamin Franklin: "Failing to plan is planning to fail."

4. In addition to deliberation, determination, self-discipline, and planning, there must be a settled belief about one's own life. It is the belief that life is not only worth living, but worth living in an improved state. Albert Camus posited if life is not worth living then suicide is the only logical course. Conversely, he believed if life is worth living then a

personally meaningful life should be pursued. Almost certain is that such a life will be punctuated by change.

Chapter V. Why Did an Eminent Psychiatrist Not Change?

How can a teacher and philosopher advise and guide others when he himself does not follow what he knows to be right?
                                                                    - Gareth Southwell

Published in 1978, Scott Peck's *The Road Less Traveled* did not become a bestseller until 1984. Eventually translated into twenty languages, over the next quarter century it sold over six million copies, making it the all-time bestselling nonfiction book with one exception - the Bible. He was listed in the *Guinness Book of World's Records* for having written the longest running book on the *New York Times* bestsellers list. *The Road Less Traveled* begins with this sentence: "Life is difficult" (1978, p. 1). From there, Peck proceeds to explain life is difficult because it consists of a series of problems, which we can moan about or solve. In addition, "the process of confronting and solving problems is a painful one" (1978, p. 16). In spite of this he is optimistic about our predicament because it has a remedy: "Discipline is the basic set of tools we require to solve life's problems. Without discipline we can solve nothing. With only some discipline we can solve only some problems. With total discipline we can solve all problems" (1978, pp. 15-16).

Sir Winston Churchill characterized the Soviet Union's foreign policy as "a riddle wrapped in a mystery, inside an enigma" (Cowell, 2008). This description also fits Dr. Peck, perhaps America's best known psychiatrist in the 1980's and 90's. In his writing he emphasized the importance and benefits of self-discipline. Yet, he admitted to a failure to rein in three behaviors in his own life:

Alcohol

I am strongly habituated to alcohol. I eagerly look forward to my gin in quite heavy doses at the end of a day. This habit has become more entrenched over the years. I dearly love the solace it brings me - the relaxation that results from having the edge taken off my consciousness - and I tend to adjust my day around the "cocktail hour" - or two or three hours (Peck, 1995, p. 43).

Smoking

Without nicotine for a couple of waking hours I become sick. For over forty years now I have used smoking, somewhat like alcohol, to provide me with brief respites from concentration and rewards for periods of hard mental work. No work requires such intense concentration as writing, and if I ever kick this fierce addiction it will probably only be at a time when I have ceased to write anymore (pp. 42-43).

Adultery

My sexual infidelity is a glaring example of the unreasonableness of romance. I would never have been diagnosed as a full-blown "sex addict," but in some ways it was surely a compulsion. A purely rational human being would have known better. I, however, am not purely rational, and this irrational part of me had to have its due. I might not have survived otherwise, but I always wished I could have been a different kind of person who did not need such an outlet. Extramarital sex is a new body and a new personality to be explored. A new territory. It is also forbidden territory, and for some that might be a turn-on. For me it never was. Whatever my psychology, the pure newness of another woman was my primary aphrodisiac (pp. 28-30).

Since Peck points to no other person or condition as the explanation for his addictions and adultery he seems to have taken responsibility for these behaviors. Concerning personal responsibility he writes, "Triggers are pulled by individuals. Orders are given and executed by individuals. In the last analysis, every single human act is ultimately the result of an individual choice" (1983, p. 215). In confessing his three failures he suggests nothing that diluted his exercise of free will. In his authorized biography, published two years after his death, he refers to these habits as volitional and views his wife Lily's decision to divorce him the result of his own doing. Nevertheless, his son, Christopher, is unimpressed by his father's confession. Shortly after Peck's death Christopher said his father was not a Jekyll and Hyde character:

because Jekyll and Hyde split himself into vice and virtue, but Scotty's virtue was really a sham. His narcissism left him a very lonely person, and his saintliness (which I found creepier than his cruelty) was a plea for love. I don't think he loved because he enjoyed loving others; he loved in order to be loved back (Jones, p. 274).

Concerning Peck's estranged relationships with his children, his biographer, Arthur Jones, writes:

Peck was indeed deeply regretting his extremely troubled relationships with his three children. Perversely, he couldn't, or rather wouldn't, admit the extent to which he was responsible for the fissures and faults that had caused the breech. An unparalleled wordsmith in conversation, he was unable or unwilling to express remorse sufficient to the damage done, in words that sincerely conveyed what he felt or ought to have felt (p. 268).

Lawsuits and criminal actions can determine responsibility and assign punishment but they cannot compel change. The determination to change emanates from the individual. Understandably, those hurt by someone's misbehavior want reassurance the behavior will not be repeated. But taking responsibility is not tantamount to committing to change. In the movie "A Civil Action," victims of irresponsible industrial waste disposal are told that perpetrators, "Say they're sorry with money" (1998). Dissatisfied with the offer of an eight million dollar settlement, the victims insist on change. They want the contaminated water wells cleansed and dumping practices discontinued. They're disappointed and bewildered by the offending corporation's simultaneous admission of wrongdoing and refusal to change.

In the New Testament the Apostle Paul writes to Christian believers at Corinth that, "Godly sorrow brings repentance" (2 Corinthians 7:10, NIV). Paul's teaching emphasizes the insufficiency of mere confession in the Christian life. He adjures those in the Corinthian church that in order for confession to be meaningful it must be accompanied by a determined effort to discontinue the unacceptable behavior. This commitment to change is captured by the Greek word *metanoia*, which means a transformative change of heart and is translated as "repent" in English. Making confession and taking responsibility, while commendable, are not enough to bring about change.

Recognizable to many who are plagued, if not tormented, by an unwanted behavior is the insufficiency of understanding for accomplishing change. Peck's understanding of human behavior in general and his own in particular were insufficient to effect the changes he said he wanted. Another psychiatrist, Dr. Szasz, addresses this insufficiency in the context of psychotherapy: "Success in psychotherapy - that is, the ability to change oneself in the direction in which one wants to change - requires courage rather than insight" (1973, p. 109).

What accounts for Dr. Peck's futility? Using chapter III ("How is change accomplished?") as a reference, this chapter addresses this brilliant, accomplished psychiatrist's failure to discontinue smoking, excessive drinking, and serial adultery.

One possibility is he gave up trying to change owing to fatigue. The renowned football coach Vince Lombardi explained the importance of conditioning to his players with the assertion, "Fatigue makes cowards of us all" (2019). Perhaps Peck, tired of trying and failing, settled for merely understanding his lack of self-discipline and might even account for why he wrote a book about it.

Regarding his adultery, Peck placed his pursuit of sensual pleasure over Lily's emotional pain. He lacked the ability to understand and share the feelings of another - a peculiar deficit for a psychiatrist. In a word, he lacked empathy, one of the five characteristics of *emotional intelligence* (Goleman, 1995). In addition to lacking empathy, he was deficient in three other components of emotional intelligence: motivation, self-regulation, and interpersonal skill. Insufficiently motivated to regulate his sensuality, it eventually sabotaged his relationship with Lily.

Lack of empathy and an inflated sense of privilege are characteristics of *narcissistic personality disorder*. Perhaps Peck's celebrity reinforced his self-perceived specialness and made him feel entitled to enjoy the "exploration" (his word) of other women. Noteworthy is that he wrote a book in which he gives considerable attention to narcissism. In *The People of the Lie* he writes,

Narcissism, or self-absorption, takes many forms. Some are more distinctly pathological than others. The subject is as complex as it is important. It is not the purpose of this book, however, to give a balanced view of the whole topic, so we will proceed immediately to that particular pathological variant that Eric Fromm called "malignant narcissism."

Malignant narcissism is characterized by an unsubmitted will. All adults who are mentally healthy submit themselves one way or another to something higher than themselves, be it God or truth or love or some other higher ideal. ... (A)ll mentally healthy individuals submit themselves to the demands of their own conscience. Not so the evil, however. In the conflict between their guilt and their will, it is the guilt that must go and the will that must win (1983, pp. 77-78).

Recall the assessment of Peck's son, Christopher: "His narcissism left him a very lonely person, and his saintliness (which I found creepier than his cruelty) was a plea for love" (Jones, p. 274). Might it be Dr. Peck had the very pathology he so eloquently described?

Another possible contributor to his frustration was his capacity for *rationalization*. As described in chapter II, rationalization is one of the Freudian defense mechanisms, operating unconsciously at defending misbehavior through flawed reasoning. He characterized smoking as indispensable to his writing; drinking as necessary for his relaxation; and adultery as possibly saving his life. Recall his explanation for adultery:

> A purely rational human being would have known better. I, however, am not purely rational, and this irrational part of me had to have its due. I might not have survived otherwise, but I always wished I could have been a different kind of person who did not need such an outlet (1995, pp. 28-29).

Peck lacked several of the conditions presented in chapter III, "How is change accomplished?" Unlike the Laura Baugh, he did not suffer any life-threatening medical consequences for his unwanted behaviors. Neither did he have an awakening experience like that of Dr. Rosenblum. And, although Peck was religiously curious and gave considerable attention to spirituality in his writing, he did not have the life-changing religious encounter of Ebenezer Scrooge or Chuck Colson.

Socrates taught reputation is what others think about a man and integrity is what a man knows about himself. Richard Kuklinski, a serial murderer who claimed to have killed over 200 people, seemed unconcerned with his reputation when he said, "I am what I am, and I don't give a flying (expletive delete) what anyone thinks of me" (Malikow, 2013, p. 41). In stark contrast to Kuklinski, Shakespeare writes of the importance of reputation: "(He) who steals my purse steals trash. ... But he that filches from me my good name robs me of that which not enriches him and makes me poor indeed" (*Othello*, Act 3, scene 3). Peck's public confession of his three unwanted behaviors does not prove he was indifferent to his reputation. But it demonstrates whatever concern he had about his reputation was insufficient to accomplish change.

The tombstone epitaph of Immanuel Kant, an 18th century German philosopher, reads, "Two things fill the mind with ever new and increasing admiration and awe, the more often and steadily we reflect upon them: the starry heavens above me and the moral law within me" (2019). These words, taken from his *Critique of Practical Reason*, communicates Kant's amazement that the Creator of the universe has an interest in his moral conduct and for this reason endowed him with a conscience. Nathaniel Hawthorne's *The Scarlet Letter* presents a powerful description of the misery that can result from a violated conscience. Set in Puritan New England, it is the story of a woman named Hester Prynne whose extramarital affair produces an illegitimate child and the public scorn that accompanies adultery. The father is Reverend Dimmesdale, the community's respected spiritual leader. Hester never discloses the identity of her lover and he lives out his years with his reputation intact. His inauthentic life, known only to Hester, is captured by the author:

> It is the unspeakable misery of a life so false as his, that it steals the pith and substance out of whatever realities there are around us, and which were meant by Heaven to be the spirit's joy and nutriment. To the

untrue man, the whole universe is false - it is impalpable - it shrinks to nothing within his grasp. And he himself, insofar as he shows himself in a false life, becomes a shadow, or, indeed, ceases to exist (1978, p. 107).

If integrity and conscience are inseparable it is reasonable to wonder if Peck lost (or never had) the restraining influence of a conscience. There is no person as dangerous to others as one whose behavior is not restricted by integrity, reputation or conscience. In an interview three years before his death, Peck gave this assessment of himself:

I don't think I ever suggested that it's good to smoke, or that people should drink or have affairs. I am not going to justify it. I've never said anywhere that they are supposed to imitate me. I've gone to great lengths not to be a guru. I think the notion of guruhood is utterly pathological, and I couldn't live that way. I am just a person. It isn't my choosing, but my fault. In a number of ways, I don't understand who I am. You can tell (the cynics) that if by some chance I am a saint, I'm the one who smokes and drinks. I'm somebody who often, like so many people, preaches what he needs to learn (Epstein, 2002).

Mencius, a Chinese philosopher who lived 24 centuries ago, would not be as generous with Peck as Peck was with himself. Mencius believed a man who does not follow his own advice is unworthy to guide others and said, "Never has a man who has bent himself been able to make others straight" (Southwell, 2018, p. 32).

Epilogue

There might be something comforting about the notion that there is, deep down, an impeccable self without disorder, and that if I try hard enough, I can reach that unblemished self. But there may be no impeccable self to reach, and if I continue to struggle toward one, I might go mad in the pursuit.

— Esme Weijun Wang

Shakespeare's *The Tragedy of Hamlet, Prince of Denmark* provides a superb analysis of how change works. Hamlet, committed to avenging the murder of his father, intensely appeals to his mother to abstain from sexual engagement with Claudius, her second husband and the murderer of Hamlet's father. Gertrude, Hamlet's mother, is so troubled by her son's accusation of Claudius that she tells her son he has broken her heart in two. He responds that she should throw away the worse half and live a purer life with the other. He continues by telling her not to go to Claudius' bed that night, implying never again to sleep with him.

Assume a virtue, if you have it not.
That monster, custom, who all sense doth eat,
Of habits devil, is angel yet in this,
That to the use of actions fair and good
He likewise gives a frock or livery
That aptly is put on. Refrain tonight,
And that shall lend a kind of easiness

To the next abstinence; the next more easy;
For use almost can change the stamp of nature.
(Act 3. scene 4).

Hamlet is urging his mother to change her behavior by pretending to be virtuous even if she's not and eventually she will no longer have to pretend. In contemporary, albeit less elegant, language Hamlet is telling her:

At least pretend to be virtuous, even if you're not.
Habit is a terrible thing, in that it's easy to get used
to doing evil without feeling bad about it. But it's also
a good thing, in that being good can also become a habit.
Say no to sex tonight, and that will make it easier to say
no the next time and still easier the time after that. Habit
can change even one's natural instincts, and even rein in
the devil in us, or kick him out (SparkNotes, 2019).

Henry Ford said, "We do not make changes for the sake of making them, but we never fail to make a change when once it is demonstrated that the new way is better than the old way" (Hoffman, 2012, p. 101). Changes in the automobile industry are not like changes in human behavior. Unlike an assembly line, people can refuse to attempt to change or fail at their attempt. Moreover, often it cannot be demonstrated beforehand that the new way is better than the old way. Sometimes the change itself provides the demonstration.

Change is more likely if the following realities are accepted as principles to be observed:

(1) *Change is difficult.* Another quotation from the fictitious *Book of Lombardi* is, "The only place success comes before work is in the dictionary" (2019).

(2) *Change requires a personal choice.* Recall the 90 percent failure rate among students in the behavioral change exercise referred to in chapter II. Commitment, a prerequisite to change, cannot be assigned - neither can necessity.

(3) *Change often requires courage.* In *The Miracle of Change* Dennis Wholey devotes an entire chapter to courage. There he quotes the political commentator Armstrong Williams: "Change is part of the fabric of humanity; and if we have already navigated some major life changes, we have probably already exhibited some courage of our own" (1997, p. 150). Recall Dr. Szasz's observation concerning the relationship between courage and success in psychotherapy: "Success in psychotherapy - that is, the ability to change oneself in the direction in which one wants to change - requires courage rather than insight" (1973, p. 109).

(4) *Change requires action.* There is a healthy kind of making believe. The colloquial version of Hamlet's prescription ("Assume a virtue if you have it not") is, "Fake it 'til you make it." Football coach Bill Parcells emphasized the

significance of action when he said, "Potential means you haven't done anything yet" (2019).

(5) *Change is a process.* "Trust the process" is a motto associated with the Philadelphia 76ers, a professional basketball team. It encourages their fans to have patience with a team engaged in a building process.

(6) *The mere passing of time does not effect change.* The adage, "With age comes wisdom" is not universally true; neither is the belief, "Time heals all wounds." While some wounds heal on their own there are others that heal only because something specific has been done with and within time.

(7) *Behaviors can be targeted and changed but rarely does a personality change.* When Heraclitus said, "All is change" he must not have had personality in mind (Southwell, 2018, p. 13). An individual's characteristic pattern of thinking, feeling, acting, and relating to others is far too complex to be subject to change. *The Big Five Personality Traits (conscientiousness, agreeableness, neuroticism, extraversion, and openness to experience) show some variability over a lifetime and in different situations. Nevertheless, since personality traits build on infant and childhood temperament they show a high degree of stability over a lifetime.*

(8) *In the rare instance of a personality change the change has occurred because of a powerful, unplanned experience or spiritual awakening.* This is not to say that all powerful, unplanned experiences or spiritual awakenings result in a personality change. Neurosurgeon Eban Alexander's bestseller, *Proof of Heaven,* recounts the near-death experience that changed his mind about the relationship between the brain and consciousness as well as the reality of an afterlife. Concerning his revised thinking he writes, "My experience showed me the death of the body and the brain are not the end of consciousness and that human experience continues beyond the grave" (2012, p. 9). But a change of mind, even about an important subject, is not a change of personality.

References

Preface

Szasz, T. (1973). *The second sin*. Garden City, NY: Anchor Press. Doubleday and Company, Inc.

Chapter I

"On deadly ground." (1994). Burbank, CA: Warner Brothers.

Popova, M. (2014). "how we become who we are: Meghan Daum on nostalgia, aging, and why we romanticize our imperfect younger selves." *brain pickings*.org. 12/09/2014.

"The Shawshank Redemption." (1994). Columbia Pictures. USA.

Townley, C. (2019). "Cosmetic surgery is on the rise, data reveal." *Medical news today*. 03/17/2019.

Wilde, O. (2019). Recovered from wisdom-but-sometimes-age-comes-alone on 04/13/2019.

Wright, R. (2017). *Why Buddhism is true: The science and philosophy of meditation and enlightenment.* New York: Simon and Schuster.

Chapter II

Eliot, T.S. (1959). *The elder statesman.* New York: Farrar, Straus and Giroux.

Horowitz, J. (2002). "Ten foods that pack a wallop." *Time magazine.* 159(3).

Malikow, M. (2014). *It's not too late: Making the most of the rest of your life (third edition).* Chipley, FL: Theocentric Publishing.

Szasz, T. (1973). *The second sin.* Garden City, NY: Anchor Press. Doubleday and Company, Inc.

Wholey, D. (1997). *The miracle of change: The path to self-discovery and spiritual growth.* "Change is hard." New York: Simon and Schuster, Inc.

Chapter III

Beaven, S. (2009). "Prominent physician dies." The Oregonian. 05/31/2009.

t 0 s e

Becker, D. (1997). "Sober Baugh vows not to break again." *USA Today*. (08/29/1997).

Burroughs, A. (2012). *This is how: Proven aid in overcoming shyness, molestation, fatness, spinsterhood, grief, disease, lushery, decrepitude & more*. New York: St. Martin's Press.

Dickens, C. (2013). *A christmas carol*. New York: Fall River Press.

Einstein, A. (1990). *The world treasure of modern religious thought*. Jeroslav Pelikan, Editor. Boston, MA: Little, Brown, and Company.

Eliot, T.S. (1959). *The elder statesman*. New York: Farrar, Straus and Giroux.

Frankl, V. (1984). *Man's search for meaning*. New York: Washington Square Press.

_____. (2006). *Man's search for meaning*. Boston, MA: Beacon Press.

Freud, S. (1982). *Civilization and its discontents*. New York: W.W. Norton and Company.

Hill, G. (1987). *The discovery bible: New american standard new testament.* Chicago. IL: Moody Press.

James, W. (1902). *The varieties of religious experience: A study in human nature.* New York: The Modern Library.

Kranz, G. (2009). *Failure is not an option: Mission control to mercury and beyond.* New York: Simon and Schuster.

Rilke, R.M. (1918). Recovered from *Ahead of all parting: Selected poetry and prose of Rainer Maria Rilke.*Translated by Stephen Mitchell. Published by Modern Library (1995).

Rosenbaum, E. (1988). *A taste of my own medicine: When the doctor is the patient.* New York: Random House.

Spence, G. (1996). *The making of a country lawyer.* New York: St. Martin's Press.

Twerski, A. (1997). *Addictive thinking: Understanding self-deception.* Center City, MN: Hazelton Publishing.

Weil, S. (1942). Letter to Father Perrin. May 26, 1942.

Chapter IV

Bennett, W. (1993). *The book of virtues. A treasury of great moral stories*. New York: Simon & Shuster.

Collins, J. (2001). *Good to great: Why some companies make the leap and others don't*. New York: Harper-Collins.

Doherty, N. (2018). "The Stockdale paradox." Recovered from http://ndoherty.com/stockdale-paradox/ on 01/03/2018.

Epictetus. (2019). Recovered from http://www.brainy quote.com/quotes/epictetus_121546.

Seligman, M. (19993). *What you can change and what you can't: The complete guide to successful self-improvement*. New York: Vintage Books. Random House.

Chapter V

"A Civil Action." (1998). Burbank, CA: Touchstone Pictures.

Cowell, A. (2008). "Churchill's definition of Russia still rings true." *The New York Times*. 08/01/2008.

Epstein, R. (2002). "M. Scott Peck: Wrestling with God." *Psychology Today*. November 2002.

Goleman, D. (1995). *Emotional intelligence: Why it matters more than i.q.* New York: Bantam Books.

Hawthorne, N. (1978). *The scarlet letter.* New York: Norton.

Kant, I. (2009). Recovered from https:www.college.columbi college.edu/core/content/kant's-tombstone-kaliningrad on *06/11/2019.*

Jones, A. (2007) *The road he traveled: The revealing biography of M. Scott Peck.* London, UK: Rider, Ebury Publishing, Random House.

Lombardi, V. (2019). Recovered from. com/quotes/vince_lombardi. 380768 on 06/05/2019.

Malikow, M. (2013). *The human predicament: Towards an understanding of the human condition.* Chipley, FL: Theocentric Publishing.

Peck, S. (1978). *The road less traveled: A new psychology of love, traditional values and spiritual growth.* New York: Touchstone. Simon and Schuster.

_____. (1983). *People of the lie: The hope for healing human evil.* New York: Simon and Schuster.

_____. (1995). *In search of stones: A pilgrimage of faith, reason, and discovery*. New York: Hyperion Books.

Southwell, G. (2018). *Philosophy in 100 quotes*. New York: Metro Books: Sterling Publishing Co., Inc.

Szasz, T. (1973). *The second sin*. Garden City, NY: Anchor Press. Doubleday and Company, Inc.

Epilogue

Alexander, E. (2012). *Proof of heaven: A neurosurgeon's journey into the afterlife*. New York: Simon and Schuster.24

Hoffman, B. (2012). *American icon: Alan Mulally and the fight to save the ford motor company*. New York: Crown Business. Random House.

Lombardi, V. (2009). Recovered from.Lombardi 109282.

Parcells, B. (2019). Recovered from http://quotefancy.com? Bill-Parcells-Potential-means-you-haven't-done-anything y... on 06/20/2019.

Southwell, G. (2018). *Philosophy in 100 quotes*. New York: Metro Books. Sterling Publishing Co., Inc.

SparkNotes (2019). Recovered from page206 on 06/12/2019.

Wholey, D. (1997). *The miracle of change: The path to self-discovery and spiritual growth.* New York Pocket Books.

About the Author

Dr. Max Malikow is on the faculty of the Renee Crown Honors Program of Syracuse University and an Adjunct Assistant Professor of Philosophy at LeMoyne College. He earned his Master's degree from Gordon-Conwell Theological Seminary and doctorate from Boston University. The author or editor of seventeen previous books, he is a practicing psychotherapist in Syracuse, New York.

Made in the USA
Middletown, DE
02 September 2019